THE

EVERYTHING KIDS' GROSS

Hidden Pictures Book

Pick your way through hours of skin-crawling fun!

Beth L. Blair

Adams Media

Avon, Massachusetts

EDITORIAL
Publishing Director: Gary M. Krebs
Associate Managing Editor: Laura M. Daly
Associate Copy Chief: Brett Palana-Shanahan
Acquisitions Editor: Kate Burgo
Associate Production Editor: Casey Ebert

PRODUCTION
Director of Manufacturing: Susan Beale
Associate Director of Production: Michelle Roy Kelly
Series Designers: Colleen Cunningham, Erin Ring
Layout and Graphics: Colleen Cunningham,
    Sorae Lee, Jennifer Oliveira
Cover Layout: Paul Beatrice, Erick DaCosta,
    Matt LeBlanc

An Everything® Series Book.
Everything® and everything.com® are registered trademarks of F+W Publications, Inc.

Published by Adams Media, an F+W Publications Company
57 Littlefield Street, Avon, MA 02322. U.S.A.
www.adamsmedia.com

ISBN 10: 1-59337-615-4
ISBN 13: 978-1-59337-615-4
Printed in the United States of America.

J I H G F E D C B

Library of Congress Cataloging-in-Publication Data
available from publisher.

This publication is designed to provide accurate and authoritative information with regard to the subject matter covered. It is sold with the understanding that the publisher is not engaged in rendering legal, accounting, or other professional advice. If legal advice or other expert assistance is required, the services of a competent professional person
should be sought.

—From a *Declaration of Principles* jointly adopted by a Committee of the
American Bar Association and a Committee of Publishers and Associations

Many of the designations used by manufacturers and sellers to distinguish their products are claimed as trademarks.
When those designations appear in this book and Adams Media was aware of a trademark claim, the designations have
been printed with initial capital letters.

Cover and interior illustrations by Kurt Dolber.
Puzzles by Beth L. Blair.

This book is available at quantity discounts for bulk purchases.
For information, call 1-800-289-0963.

See the entire Everything® series at *www.everything.com*.

Dedication

To Dr. Finkelstein and Monsieur Joseph Pujol—you are my heroes!
To all the editors at Adams—you are saints!
BLB

Contents

Goodness, Grossness!

Believe it or not, gross is much more than just farts, vomit, and poop! People all around you do gross things every day—sometimes their job is gross, sometimes their food is gross, and sometimes they think gross is an adventure!

So in this book I decided to take a closer, and grosser, look at all kinds of people who make gross stuff a big part of their day. You may never actually meet these people, but by the end of this book, you're going to feel very close to them. In fact, you're going to be searching for spiders in their salads and picking up their smelly socks.

What? Well, what did you think? This is a gross hidden picture book! You've got to get up close and personal with these folks and find out exactly what it is that makes them special, and especially gross. So sharpen your pencil and your detective skills, and go dig out the gross!

Start hunting in the kitchen, sniffing out cooks who serve up fried tarantula, jellyfish salad, and maggot cheese. Check out the "raw bar" where food is served alive, and then search for edible ears at the "barf buffet" where all the food looks really dead. Keep looking and you'll find the tallow candles that hungry explorers found good enough to eat!

It may take a bit of time travel, but you'll crawl through a Greek wrestling match to pick up the extra eyeballs, track down the dice swallowed by gamblers back in Olde England, and try trapping ravenous rats in the hold of a wooden pirate ship. While you're down there, will ye ferret out the foul smells coming up from the bilge?

Think scientists always work in nice, clean laboratories? Nope! You're going to follow them outside and dig through a landfill for dirty diapers, beat the bushes to pick up ticks, and wade through the jungle to collect ape pee (try not to get wet)!

Finally, you'll be right there with daring doctors who sniff smelly mouths to study bad breath, and pry open skulls to check out the brain . . . while the patient is still awake! You'll be looking for leeches, finding fingers, and discovering a heap of weird stuff swallowed by dogs! And since you can never quite get away from poops, you'll be measuring piles of those, too.

Yup, from the crafty pioneers who insulated their cabins with manure, to cutting-edge creative artists who use stinky garbage to create their art, you'll be finding the hidden gross in people and places where you just never thought to look!

Good luck,
happy hunting,
and get ready to
GET GROSSED OUT!

–Beth L. Blair

PS. I assure you that
the only gross habit I
I have is writing gross
books!

Chapter 1

Gross Athletes

Ready, Set, Go?

Cyclists in a long race eventually have to pee. Some riders hop off the bike, but others don't want to waste the time. They just pee as they peddle! Can you find the 12 items that got sprayed as this group sped by? Look for a soda bottle, milk pitcher, teacup, kite, postage stamp, mug, pair of scissors, acorn, bowling pin, ice cream cone, vase with flowers, and sailboat.

P.S. How many of these items can hold water?

Rough Landing

Motocross riders have to be tough, because when things go wrong during a jump 100 feet in the air—SPLAT! It seems like these athletes are treated by mechanics, not doctors. Badly broken bones are held together with metal rods, plates, and screws!

Can you find the 20 bones hidden in this picture? You better find them fast—looks like this rider might need a few replacements!

Play Ball!

"Bat boys" do more than just carry bats—they are the behind-the-scenes grunts of baseball. They scrub the spit-covered dugout, pick up sweaty uniforms, empty trash, vacuum, and clean all the players' cleats. But it's all worth the chance to be part of the tradition in some clubhouses: players line up to spit on the shoes of the new bat boys!

The bat boys can't leave until they find the 11 dirty socks in this locker room.

Gross Athletes

Throw the Dice

Throwing dice to gamble isn't actually a sport, but the players do have a history of being quick on their feet. In the 1700s, men who ran illegal gambling houses hired a special person to swallow the dice if the police showed up. No dice, no game, no arrest! There's no record of how the players got the dice back after the cops left.

Can you find the 16 hidden dice?

Row, Row, Row Your Boat

Long distance rowers need heavy calluses to protect their hands from the oars. At first, their hands just blister. Then, the blisters burst and new blisters form underneath. After about 15 days of steady rowing, blistering, bursting, and oozing, the rower has a good set of calluses. Believe it or not, this is the easy part. It's the rower's poor butt that really hurts!

Can you find the nine unblistered hands?

Blood & Sweat

Pro wrestlers used to use hidden razor blades to cut their foreheads. Even tiny cuts would bleed like crazy. Blood would mix with the sweat pouring down the wrestler's face to make a truly gory picture.

Can you find the word SWEAT five times and the word BLOOD six times?

Lunch Overboard!

Extreme speed plus huge waves can make even the most experienced ocean racer turn green. During a big storm, most of the crew might be yakking over the rail. But with a 70-foot long sailboat to handle, barfing sailors still have do their job!

Can you find eleven items from lunch that got "tossed"?

Gross Athletes

Seeing Red

Ultramarathon runners run in races of 50 miles or more! These athletes have to be very careful to drink enough water. If they don't, the inside of their bladder can get so dried out that the sides rub together until it's scraped, raw, and bloody. The runners know this has happened when their pee turns dark red. Not a good sign!

Runner #3 has two water bottles strapped to his hands. Can you find 12 others?

Uncle!!

Modern pro wrestling is carefully scripted so, most of the time, no one really gets hurt. But the ancient Greeks were not so polite. Back then, a popular event was the "pankration," a mix of wrestling and kickboxing. The only rule was that you couldn't gouge out an opponent's eyes. However, one well-known athlete was famous for holding his rivals and breaking their fingers!

Find 10 new eyes for the wrestler who is being gouged.

Round and Round You Go

A "Zorbonaut" is strapped into a ten-foot round, clear plastic ball (the Zorb), and then rolled down a steep hill. For a real thrill, 15 gallons of water can be thrown into the Zorb, too. The question is, what happens if the Zorbonaut throws up in there?

Find 10 other "rounds" in this picture: inline skate, donut, tennis ball, top, diamond ring, boomerang, pinwheel, yoyo, clock, and planet.

Bubble Trouble

The German swim team once tried a unique method to give their athletes a boost. Swimmers had several liters of air pumped into their bodies where farts usually come out! This extra air was supposed to help them float more easily. However, this treatment was banned before the 1976 Olympics.

Can you find nine anchors to help weigh these swimmers down again?

Chapter 2
Gross Explorers

Space Poop

During a spacewalk, an astronaut can't slip inside and use the bathroom. That's why one of the layers of a space suit is a giant diaper! Phew—now there aren't any poops orbiting the Earth!

Find the 10 items that are NOT space poop. Look for a light bulb, cowboy hat, toothbrush, hot dog in bun, sock, coat hanger, roll of TP, capital letter E, banana, and candy cane. Oh, all right . . . you can look for one piece of floating poop!

Foul Fugitives

In 1805 when Pierre Bruneseau began to explore the Paris sewer system, he wasn't sure what he'd find. He found a lot of poop, of course, and the skeletons of a few escaped zoo animals. But Pierre was really surprised to discover that the sewers were a favorite hideout for criminals on the run!

Can you find the nine crooks hiding in this sewer?

Candlelight Supper?

Exploring the Louisiana Territory with Lewis and Clark wasn't easy. At one point, the expedition ran out of supplies and had to eat one of their horses. After that, they drank bear oil from the lamps. Actually, Lewis had brought emergency dried food he called "portable soup." The other explorers thought it was so gross, they ate a case of candles instead!

Can you find 15 candles for these hungry guys?

Headaches

After exploring the world in search of gold, Sir Walter Raleigh returned to England to spend time with his family. He almost got his wish. King James charged Sir Walter with treason, and had him beheaded. Raleigh's head was embalmed and given to his wife. For 29 years she carried it with her everywhere!

Help Sir Walter to find the word GOLD 10 times.

Rock Snot

In 1999 cavers discovered something strange as they explored deep in a Mexican cave. Nicknamed "snotties" because they are white, squishy, and hang from the ceiling of the cave, these formations are actually alive. Stranger still, the snotties ooze a liquid acid so strong, it ate holes in the explorers' shirts!

Can you find the 16 other snots in this cave? They all look sort of like this:

Gross Explorers

Dinner Duo

In 1914, explorer Ernest Shackleton led an expedition across Antarctica. Unfortunately, the ice crushed his ship. While the crew waited to be rescued they ate two things: seal and penguin. When they got tired of that, they had only two other things to eat: penguin and seal!

Find the explorers something else to eat: a fried egg, ice cream cone, banana, slice of watermelon, bunch of grapes, and a piece of bacon. Just in case, you better find two other penguins and four other seals, too!

Yank!

Daniel Boone was a crafty woodsman who helped to explore and settle the state of Kentucky. At one point, he was captured and adopted into the Shawnee tribe. But the adoption ceremony wasn't easy. Daniel had all the hair on his head plucked out, one hair at a time, except for one small tuft on top!

Can you find the gifts Daniel got from his new family? BOOT, HORSE, AX, TEEPEE, RIFLE, HORSESHOE, PITCHER.

Head for Gold

Many explorers searching for the Lost Dutchman Mine in Arizona never made it home. Over time, the skeletons of these prospectors have been discovered scattered throughout the hills. The strange thing is, at least five of them have been found missing their heads!

Can you find the six skulls and five long bones hiding in them thar hills?

Snow Burn

Explorers who scale mountain peaks often climb across shiny white fields of snow. All this work makes them gasp for breath in the thin air. That's the perfect way to get a terrible sunburn on the roof of the mouth! Sunlight shining off the snow can also scorch inside the nostrils.

Find 11 ice cream cones to chill this climber's burn.

Oh, Nuts!

When "urban explorers" poke through abandoned mines, they face big dangers like chemicals, explosives, and toxic fumes. But there are tiny dangers, too. Just walking through an old mine can knock loose small rocks. After falling a few hundred feet, these mini missiles—no bigger than a peanut—can smash right through an unprotected skull!

Can you find the 14 peanut-sized rocks hidden in this mine before they find the explorer's head?

Not with Your Mouth Full!

Find the four words that make up the answer to the following riddle:

What did the cannibal say to the explorer?

____ _____ ____ ___!

Rat Ho!

Pirate ships were stuffed with casks full of food, enough to last months at sea. No wonder they were also crawling with rats! Rats ate the food, chewed the boat, and sometimes even nibbled on the pirates. You can see why rat hunting was a popular hobby. Legend has it that one ship trapped over 4,000 rats!

Can you find 16 rats bunking in with the pirates?

Glub, Glub!

What happened to a pirate who stole from a shipmate, or refused to fight? The worst punishment was to be "marooned," or left alone on a tiny spit of land in the middle of nowhere. These mini islands were often only visible at low tide. But a few hours later, the abandoned pirate could be up to his neck in water!

Was this pirate left empty handed? Find the following useful items: pot, fried egg, banana, spoon, three matches, needle and thread, slice of pizza, cutlass, sailboat, drink with a straw, rope, fishhook, slice of bacon, scoop of ice cream, pair of flippers!

Captain No Nose

Pirate Captain Edward Low was known to be savage and cruel. His favorite little "joke" was to cut off the nose or ears of his prisoners!

Can you find the 10 times the word NO is hidden in this portrait of Captain Low?

Nasty Nines

To keep order on the ship, a Pirate Captain would have a mis-behaving pirate "flogged." A whip was made from a piece of rope unraveled into nine strands with a knot on the tip of each strand. This terrible tool was called the "cat o' nine tails." After the flogging, salt water was thrown on the pirate's bloody back. This stung so bad, it was often worse than being beaten!

Find the nine number 9s and the nine word NINEs.

Hard Life

Pirates ate a lot of "hardtack," a rock-hard cracker made from flour and water. After months at sea, the hardtack would be full of worms, weevils, and maggots. Pirates had to eat it anyway! Smart pirates would crumble their hardtack into a hot drink. The bugs would float to the top and could be skimmed off!

Look for the 13 bugs and the 9 worms hiding in these pirates' dinners.

Fish Food

A captured pirate was usually hanged. Then the body would be locked in a metal cage and displayed as a warning to other pirates. The favorite place for this grim message was at the entrance to a harbor. This made getting rid of the rotten pirate easy—the cage was opened and the pieces thrown to the fish!

Find the 14 hidden fish waiting for their pirate dinner!

Cut on the Dotted Line

You would think the ship's carpenter and the surgeon would be different pirates. But sometimes they were the same person. Why? The carpenter had the sharp tools needed to amputate an arm or leg, and knew how to cut quickly!

Can you find the 10 saws hidden in the "surgeon's" shop?

Bilge Rats

Wooden pirate ships were always leaking. Water would seep into the very bottom of the boat, or "bilge." Tiny sea creatures that came in with the water would die and rot, causing the bilge to stink like sewage. Pumping the bilges was a disgusting job saved for the "bilge rats," or pirates being punished.

Can you find the following smelly words? FETOR, FOUL, STENCH, STINK, GROSS, REEK, PUTRID, FECAL, ROTTEN.

Oops!

What happens if a pirate comes at you with an ax? You have an ax-i-dent!

Can you find the nine hidden axes in this picture?

Move Over

Everyone likes privacy when using the bathroom, especially when pooping! But there was no privacy for a pirate. The bathroom was usually a board hanging over the water near the bow of the ship. Holes in the board let the poops fall right in the ocean. There were often two holes or more!

Can you find the six rolls of TP and the five sheets of newspaper in this open-air bathroom?

Smile?!

Pirates didn't eat a lot of fresh fruits and veggies on their long sea trips. That's why many of them had a nasty disease called "scurvy." First the pirates would get black and blue spots on their skin. Next, their gums would bleed. Finally, their teeth would fall out!

ARRRRR! Citrus fruit will help cure these scurvy dogs! Can you find the 12 lemons in this picture?

Chapter 4

Gross Doctors

WAIT! I Want a Haircut!

Hundreds of years ago, people went to the barber if they needed a haircut, but also if they needed a tooth pulled! Unfortunately, these barber/dentists didn't know about anesthesia. It took several strong men to hold down the patient!

Can you find 19 teeth this barber pulled today?

HAIR CUT 25¢

tooth pul'd 50¢

Open Wide

"Trepanning" is an operation where a doctor cuts a flap of scalp, folds it back, and then drills or cuts a hole in the skull to relieve pressure on the brain. You would think this would be done in an operating room with high-tech instruments. Surprise! This surgery was being performed as long as 4,000 years ago, with the patient wide awake!

Can you find the picture of a skull with a hole cut into it?

Slimy Helpers

It's tricky to reattach a finger or ear that's been cut off in an accident. The hard part is getting blood to flow through the sewn-on part. Doctors sometimes get help from special "living" pumps. These pumps work great, but why are they gross? Because they are bloodsucking leeches!

Can you find the 10 leeches that are loose in the lab?

Instant Finger, Just Add Toe

If you had to choose a body part that looks like a finger, what would it be? A toe! Even though they are shorter and stubbier, toes have the same basic parts as fingers. So, if someone loses a finger in an accident, doctors can amputate a toe, and move it to the person's hand. Instant finger!

Can you find the 10 cut-off fingers hiding in this picture?

Peculiari-tea

In certain regions of China, traditional doctors use a special tea to treat the flu, diarrhea, nosebleeds, and heatstroke. What's so gross about a cup of tea? This tea is brewed from caterpillar poop!

Can you find the nine cups of "worm tea" in this doctor's office?

Totally Tumors

The *Guinness Book of World Records* lists a man who has had the greatest number of operations ever. Most of the surgeries were to remove tumors on his face. So, how many operations are we talking about? Did you guess 100? Or maybe 300? Try 970 operations!

Can you find the 15 needles and thread the doctors used to stitch this man up again?

Potty Mouth

Can you find the five hidden words that finish this joke? Write them on the dotted lines.

Bark and Barf

A veterinarian is a doctor that treats animals instead of people. Dogs in particular have a habit of eating things they shouldn't, and vets often have to "go in" and remove a disgusting assortment of garbage. How disgusting? How about a dog that swallowed an entire dead, and very rotten, porcupine?

Find the following items that have been eaten by dogs: LADY'S SHOE, KNIFE, ROPE, BOOT, WRISTWATCH, PENCIL, COMB, LIGHTBULB, THUMBTACK, SOCK, MITTEN, SPATULA.

Eye Doctor

A "cataract" happens when the clear lens in your eye gets cloudy. This makes it difficult to see because everything looks foggy. Today your eye doctor would replace the old lens with a new plastic lens. But if you lived in ancient Egypt, the doctor would mix the brains of a tortoise with honey and put that in your eye. Much easier!

Can you find the 13 eyes hidden in this picture?

Bug Bites

A thousand years ago, adhesive bandages did not exist. How did a doctor close a cut in the skin? One way was to find a certain kind of ant that had big pincers. The doctor held the edges of the wound, and got the ant to pinch it closed. Then the doctor cut off the head of the ant! The heads would stay until the skin grew together again.

Can you find the five ancient ant heads and the five modern adhesive bandages hidden in this picture?

Gross Anatomy

All student doctors take a class called "gross anatomy." In this case, gross doesn't mean disgusting. It means studying body parts that are big enough to see without a microscope. What about organs that are buried deep inside? Donated cadavers (dead bodies) are carefully taken apart piece by piece. By the end of the class, everything that was hidden inside the body has been taken out and studied.

These students will soon see a real heart. Until they do, help them find the 15 heart shapes hidden in this classroom.

Chapter 5
Gross Warriors

Ouch!

A caltrop is made of sharp metal spikes arranged so that one sharp point always sticks up. This simple weapon has been used since Roman times to slow down approaching soldiers, horses, and even war elephants. That's because it's hard to fight if there's a sharp metal thing stuck in your foot!

Can you find the 11 times the word OUCH shows up in this battle scene?

Gross Warriors

Great Grease!

The warriors of ancient Japan believed they had powerful protection from the knives and swords of their enemies. Was it a new kind of helmet? A super suit of armor? Nope—they smeared themselves with a grease made from squished toads!

This warrior is now protected. Can you find the 11 daggers that can no longer pierce him?

ARE YOU DONE YET?

Battle Scars

During a battle, a knight depended on his squire. Dropped sword? The squire handed him a new one. Knocked off his horse? The squire helped him remount. Cut with a sword and the wound won't stop bleeding? The trusty squire would take a red-hot knife blade, and burn the wound closed. Thanks!

Can you find the 20 burning matches the squire used to light the fire?

Dirty Laundry

By the end of a long battle, the outside of a knight's armor was covered with mud and blood. The inside was filled with sweat, blood, and even poop! It was the squire's job to make sure the armor was clean for the next fight. Water was precious, so this lucky guy used sand, vinegar, and urine to scrub off the gunk.

Find the words MUD, BLOOD, SWEAT, POOP and URINE, two times each!

Ready, Aim, THROW!

The trebuchet was a tool used by warriors for a thousand years. Its long throwing arm and heavy sling made it perfect for throwing rocks at the enemy. Sometimes more disgusting ammunition was used. Battlefield debris came in handy, including dead animals and sometimes even severed heads.

Can you find 15 incredibly smelly socks for this army to throw?

Soldier's Soup

Spartans were warriors of ancient Greece known for being tough. For example, soldiers-in-training weren't given enough to eat so that they would learn how to steal food. Unfortunately, one of the famous foods of Sparta was soup made from vinegar and pig's blood. Stealing it might make you tough, but eating it? Ugh!

Find these soldiers some better grub. Look for HOT DOG IN A BUN, PIECE OF PIZZA, BOWL OF NOODLES, CARROT, SLICE OF BREAD, CHICKEN LEG, FISH, MUSHROOM SLICE, and a FORK.

Wild Warriors

The fiercest Viking warriors were the "berserkers." Before a battle, these fighters would paint their faces, howl like animals, jump around, and bite their shields. When they were totally wound up, the berserkers would charge the enemy wearing just a bearskin!

Today we use the word *berserk* to mean crazy. Can you find the 9 CRAZY and 10 WILD words in this picture?

Gross Warriors
Food Bag

Civil War soldiers carried their food in a canvas bag called a "haversack." Since this was way before the invention of aluminum foil or plastic wrap, meat, coffee, hard biscuits, and any other food were all thrown in the sack together. If he was lucky, a soldier would have a scrap of rubber to wrap his coffee in, to keep the meat grease out of it!

Can you find 10 cups of coffee to help these soldiers wash down their dubious dinner?

There She Blows!

The first military sub-marines were not very high tech. Even flushing the toilet was tricky! Compressed air was used to blast the toilet's load out of the sub. Since the bubbles might give away the sub's position, toilets were only flushed at night. If you turned the wrong valve, a day's worth of poop would blow into the sub!

Can you find the seven horrified faces hiding in the blow up?

Gross Warriors
Clean Machine?

Soldier Keller was ordered to clean the dirty garbage cans in the mess hall. "In this day and age, the army should have a machine to clean these cans!" complained Keller. "They do," answered the sergeant. "You are its latest model!"

Ha, ha! Can you find the 10 scrub brushes and 2 toothbrushes hiding in this mess? Pvt. Keller gets to clean one less garbage can for each coat hanger you find.

What's the Rush?

Fighter pilots need super skills to maneuver their speedy aircraft. They also need super pants! When a pilot zips through a sharp turn, the blood in his or her body is pushed down to their feet. Guess what? Without enough blood in the head, the pilot passes out! Special pants squeeze the pilot's legs and guts to keep the blood up where it's needed.

"G" forces are how many times more than normal gravity is squeezing a pilot in a sharp turn. Find the G's to see how squashed this pilot is now.

Wiggly Dinner

While some people smack spiders, other people snack on spiders! This man is eating a tasty fried tarantula. Can you find the rest of his meal? Look for a snail, scorpion, ant, jellyfish, worm, caterpillar, and whale. For dessert he had a pear, a banana, and an ice cream cone. He'll need a knife and a fork, too!

Peanut Butter and Jellyfish

Most people at the beach yell "EEEEEW GROSS! Jellyfish!" But some people actually like jellyfish—to eat. It might not taste like much, but cooks use jellyfish because of its unique texture. They have nicknamed it "rubber bands"!

Can you find the 11 jellyfish and 8 peanuts hidden at the beach?

2 Scoops of Goop

We all scream for ice cream, right? What if the choice was lobster or haddock ice cream? No? How about chocolate/garlic, or bacon/egg. Still no? Ah, you must want the seal oil, reindeer fat, and berries ice cream! Believe it or not, these are all real ice cream flavors that people can buy. Depending on where you live, of course!

Can you find the 12 fried eggs this ice cream man needs for tomorrow's special flavor?

Gross Cooks

Barf Buffet

Imagine the following buffet choices: Used Litterbox Casserole, Chopped Brain Salad, Poppin' Pimples, and Slimy Eyeballs. Would you feel more hungry if you knew the recipes used hamburger and rice, gelatin and cottage cheese, tomatoes and cream cheese, and peeled grapes? Maybe, but the cooks who invented these dishes made sure the food looks just as gross as it sounds. Dig in!

Can you find 15 "edible ear" appetizers, plus 3 forks for extra guests?

Glue Broth

Hundreds of years ago, travelers would cook up a pot of meaty "glue broth" before leaving home. They would boil meat, bones, and pig's feet together, and let the broth cool into a rubbery hunk of meat-flavored gelatin. Later, they just added boiling water, and had instant soup. Why the strange name? Pig's feet were also an important ingredient in furniture maker's glue!

Count all the pig's feet and the bones you can find. More feet than bones makes good, gluey broth!

Gross Cooks

On Top of Spaghetti?

When mountain climbing, all of your energy goes toward putting one foot in front of the other. There isn't much energy left to fix fancy meals. Toward the end of the climb, tired cooks come up with some pretty gross food combos. How about yesterday's ravioli that's frozen into your cup, with this morning's hot chocolate dumped in on top of it?

Give these guys a break—find 14 ice cream cones for them!

Slow Cooking

Be careful if you go to dinner in a restaurant where you don't understand the language. You might think you know what you have ordered, but if a French waiter sets a plate of escargot (ess-car-GO) on the table, you're going to be eating snails! Bon appétit!

Can you find the 13 snails that have escaped from the kitchen?

Wanted Alive

There is one gross food that isn't cooked at all. In fact, it is eaten while it's still alive! Yup, clams are still breathing when the diners at a "raw bar" slurp them out of the shell. As an extra bonus, the contents of the clam's stomach contain bacteria, viruses, and other gunk the clam has sucked up from the bottom of the sea. Pass the lemon!

Four clams is not enough for this guy. Can you find him six more clams in their shells?

Scones with Slime

The hagfish has the gross nickname of "slime eel" because it makes gobs of goopy slime to get rid of predators. Some students who were visiting a marine science center wondered if the slime had other uses. It sure looked like egg whites. . . . So they tried slime instead of eggs to bake a batch of scones. It worked! Would you try one?

Can you find SLIME nine times?

Worm Cheese

Do you think moldy blue cheese is gross? What about cheese with maggots? In the Sardinian region of Italy, *casu marzu* (rotten cheese) is a local delicacy. The cheese makers let flies lay eggs in a piece of hard cheese. The *casu marzu* is ready when it's soft and squishy, stinks, and is full of wiggling maggots. A word of warning: the maggots tend to shoot out of the cheese toward your face. Some Sardinians suggest eating *casu marzu* with a hand over the eyes!

Can you find the 15 non-cheese-eating earthworms hiding with their maggot friends?

Sneaky Salad

The sneezeguards at the supermarket salad bar work at keeping snot out of the lettuce, but how about all the shoppers that sneak a taste of cheese or a piece of ham? Where have those fingers been, and have they been washed recently? Ick!

Are those bacon bits? NO! Find the 15 creepy crawlies that have dropped into this salad. There are three other no-no's in here, too. What are they?

A Stitch in Time

"Mountain men" were the first pioneers to explore the West. They had to be tough since they traveled and hunted alone. How tough were they? Well, Jedediah Smith was attacked by an angry bear. He sewed on his own scalp after the bear had ripped it off!

Help Jedediah find a knife, a pair of scissors, two thimbles, and seven needles with thread.

Well, at least that bear made me a nice coat!

Sea Sick?

Covered wagons didn't have shock absorbers, so they would lurch and heave over every bump in the trail. Since the trail was mostly a rutted track made from wagons that had gone before, it was really bumpy. It was not unusual for pioneers who rode in the wagon to get seasick!

Pioneers left more than just their lunch along the trail! Can you find a pair of boots, pair of socks, two teacups, thimble, umbrella, hanger, and ladle?

Packed with Poop

To keep their cabins warm, early pioneers stuffed the cracks between the logs with small stones or wood chips. Then they would "daub" on a mixture of straw, clay, and cow or buffalo poop to fill the holes!

Can you find the other items this pioneer has used as insulation? Look for a saw, ruler, shovel, quill, pitcher, arrow, comb, knife, broom, spoon, sock, toothbrush, hatchet, candle, needle and thread, fishhook, and pencil.

Gross, but true!

The best recipe for daubing: equal parts clay soil and manure. Add handfuls of chopped hay, and mix with your feet.

Gross Pioneers

Packed with People

If a weary traveler came by, a pioneer family would have company for the night. This was in addition to the mom and dad, their kids, an aunt and uncle and their kids, maybe a grandma, and the visiting preacher. Imagine all these people spending the night in a cabin no larger than your living room!

The cabin is also packed with everyone's stuff! Can you find a teacup, ladle, baby's T-shirt, log, kite, pair of dice, clock, sock, needle and thread, and toothbrush?

Wicked Water

Pioneer families wanted to have water nearby, so they would dig a well close to the cabin. Unfortunately, they also wanted the outhouse, chicken coop, and horse barn close by, too. The poop from all the people and animals would seep into the ground and turn the fresh water into a nasty brew. Most well water needed to be boiled before being used!

Can you find the 10 bottles of fresh water?

Hmmm... Water's a little thick today.

Good to the Last Drop

If a pioneer family hauled water to fill the bathtub, they didn't use it just once! First the entire family would bathe. Then they would use the water to "clean" the house or do heavy laundry. Finally the water was thrown on the garden, or dripped on the dirt floor to help keep down the dust.

While you're in there here's the baby to wash and scrub these pants, too, OK? And here's the frying pan from last night and the spoons need

Can you find 10 other hidden objects for this dad to wash? Look for one T-shirt, two socks, three mugs, and four spoons.

Poopsicles

An outhouse sitting over a hole filled with poop from an entire family was incredibly stinky in the heat of summer. But while the "privy" sure smelled better during the winter, there were other problems. Poop froze almost immediately and the pile quickly reached right up to the seat. Creative pioneers kept a shovel or other tool within reach to knock the pile down before adding to it!

Can you help this poor pioneer find eight hidden shovels?

Flied Chicken

Most pioneers' cabins didn't have screens for the windows, so flies attracted to the stinky outhouse easily got inside the house. A common chore was to have a child wave a small branch over the dinner table while the family ate. This kept most of the flies away!

Can you find the 13 FLYs that made it past the kid with the stick?

Secret Ingredient

Turning a hairy animal hide into a wearable shirt is a big, smelly job. After all the meaty bits have been scraped off the hide, it's soaked with urine to loosen the hair. Then the hair is scraped off, and the hide is rubbed with some kind of fat. Fish oil and beef fat can be used, but there's another ingredient that works even better. This gushy animal part should be cooked into a kind of soup, and used while still hot. Can you guess what it is? Here's a hint: It is smart to use this ingredient when making leather!

Look for the five hidden letters below that spell out the secret ingredient for making good leather!

House Call

A pioneer family did not often call a doctor, so every family had a few favorite remedies. To help a sore throat, a piece of moldy bread would be soaked in water, and the mold-water would be used to gargle. Or the person with a cold would have their chest rubbed with goose grease and kerosene!

Can you find 15 items you might use if you had a sore throat? Look for three each of aspirin tablets, thermometers, lemon slices, spoons for honey, and mugs hot for tea.

The Clean Plate Club

Most pioneer families had so little fresh water that every drop was precious. If you did a good job cleaning your plate, with either your spoon, a piece of bread, or your tongue, no water would have to be used to wash it. Just be sure you got your same plate next meal!

The boys are going fishing after all their hard work. How many worms can you find for them? Can you find the 13 hidden fish?

Chapter 8

Gross Scientists

Sneak Peek

How do scientists study how cows digest? They make a hole in the cow's side, and connect a wide tube to the stomach. There's a plug in the end of the tube. When the scientist wants to take a look, he or she uncorks the hole, reaches inside, and pulls out . . . well, basically a handful of half-digested cow food. But hey, that's science!

There are some strange food samples hiding in this cow. Look for an asparagus spear, bacon slice, muffin, fried egg, piece of Swiss cheese, pear, peanut, slice of bread, candy cane, bagel, fish, piece of pizza, and glass of juice with a straw.

Dooo yoooou mind?

Totally Tubular

To study the giant "tube worm," scientists collect the tubes and cut them open to measure the worms inside. Sounds easy until you know the worms are up to three feet long, flinch when they are grabbed, and bleed like crazy if they are accidentally nicked with the knife. Sometimes it's easier to just squeeze the worm out of the tube like bright red toothpaste!

Can you find the 10 toothbrushes hiding with the tube worms?

Finally!

After many years of testing and observation, scientists have finally discovered the difference between roast pork and pea soup!

Can you find the four-word answer to this silly science stumper? Write the words in the correct order on the dotted lines provided.

Excuse You!

Some scientists study mysteries such as whale migration. And some scientists study herrings farting! They haven't figured out yet why the fish do it, but they squeeze air out of their swim bladders at night. Is it a social thing? Is it a defense thing? What lucky scientist gets to find out?

A herring fart sounds a bit like a bugle. Can you find the 12 bugles these scientists are listening to?

Digging for Diapers

Listen to this: "An archaeological study of garbage from 1977 to 1985 found that disposable diapers made up about 1 percent of the solid waste in landfills." Hmmm . . . Archeologists dig through layers of history, right? So the scientists studying disposable diapers actually had to dig through the landfill and measure the amount of really old, decomposing diapers they found. What a job!

Help dig through this landfill to find 15 disposable diapers. Five of them are supersized!

The Nose Knows

If you're a scientist who studies bad breath, you've got to go right in where the stink is made. You're going to be sniffing foul mouths, and scraping the crud off brown, crusty tongues. You might even massage infected tonsils and then smell what oozes out. Yup, bad breath is seriously gross science!

Can you find the 12 not-smiley faces that are hiding from all this bad breath?

BEWARE BROWN SPOTS

3X

BRC

Bathroom 101

There is an architect who wrote a book about designing better bathrooms. Along the way, he found all kinds of gross facts about what actually goes on in a bathroom. For example, "The average human poop is about 8 inches long and weighs between 3 and 7 ounces." Now, some doctor or scientist had to measure and weigh a LOT of poops to be able to say that!

Can you find the numbers 3 through 7, two times each?

Gross Scientists

Look Out Below!

Scientists can't get too close when studying endangered apes. So how can they learn if the animals are healthy? They stand underneath and wait for them to pee! The urine can be analyzed, the ape is undisturbed, and the scientist gets just a little wet (unless it's a really big ape). Good deal!

There's a lot of peeing going on in this jungle! Can you find 16 capital letters P?

Rot Watch

A body at a crime scene is an important clue. How long has it been there? To come up with a timeline, scientists take donated cadavers, set them outside, and wait for them to decompose. Every day they check the bodies carefully, and take notes. And every night, they take a lot of showers!

Can you find the 11 hidden skulls these scientists have studied?

Come and Get It!

Some scientists collect bloodsucking ticks to study. One way to do this is to drag a white sheet through tall grass and bushes. Then they pick all the ticks off the sheet. The scientists need to be careful picking off any ticks that have bitten into them. Disease-carrying ticks can barf bad bacteria into the tick bite as they are being pulled out!

How many ticks can you find lurking in this forest?

The Vomit Comet

This page isn't upside down—it's the scientists who are topsy turvey! To learn about outer space, scientists need to experiment in zero gravity. They do this by taking a special plane very high, very fast, and then letting it free fall for thousands of feet. This makes the scientists weightless, but it also makes them barf!

Can you find the 10 places where there is VOMIT?

Chapter 9

Gross Artists

Hairy Portrait

If someone has lost a beloved pet, they can send clippings of the animal's hair to a special artist. He or she will make a picture of the pet using hair instead of paint! Some artists use human hair, too.

Can you find 10 other items in this portrait of a poodle? Look for a collar and tag, stick, tennis ball, squeaky mouse, bone, fluffy slipper, leash, chicken drumstick, and a cat (head only!). Gross artist—she included a pile of poodle doo, too!

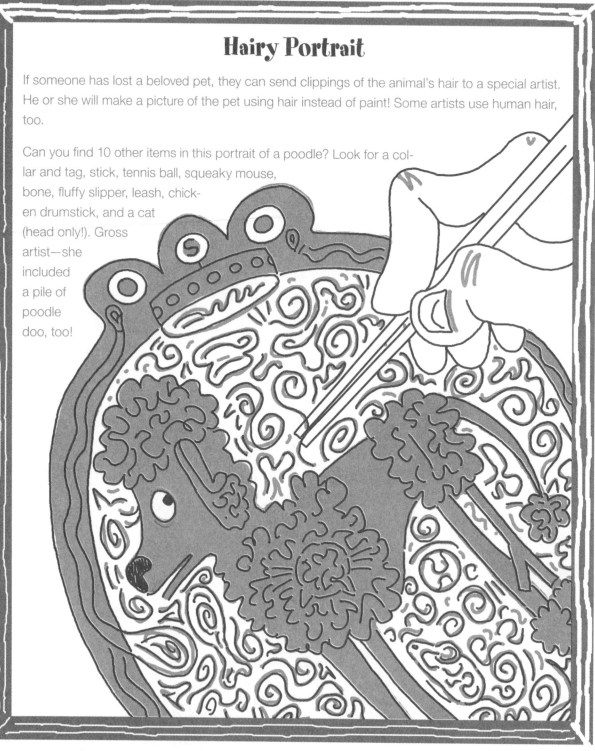

Petite Feet

Wealthy Chinese women of the tenth century were living works of art. It took two years, several broken toes, and a lot of tight bandages, but in the end the women would have tiny feet, some just three inches long! The foot itself looked like a hoof and was terribly painful, but most people only saw the fantastic embroidery on the ladies' slippers.

Find the 17 OUCHes.

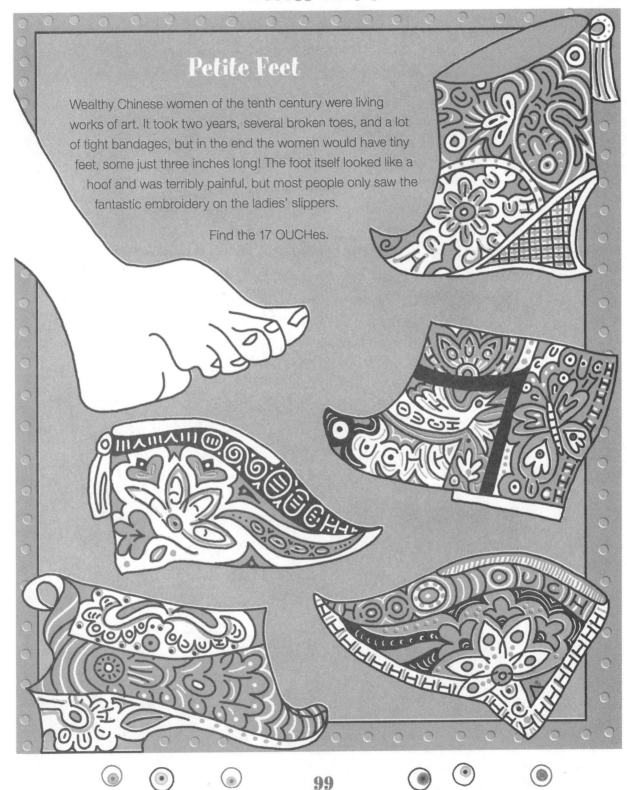

Play It Again, Slime

"Slime molds" are strange living things that grow like mushrooms but can also slither like slugs. A biologist noticed slime molds pulsing in and out, sometimes fast, and sometimes slow. He translated these rhythms into slime mold music! One common slime mold has the descriptive nickname "yellow dog vomit." Imagine how that music sounds!

Can you find the 15 hidden music notes?

So Lifelike!

There's an artist whose sculptures are made from real bodies! He has found a way to replace all the water and fat with plastic, creating a modern mummy that is flexible and rot-free. Some people think this artist is gross because he peels the plasticized people apart to show how the muscles look in action.

Can you find these 17 plastic items? False eye, comb, toothbrush, soda bottle, straw, credit card, flashlight, boot, watch, ruler, cup, cell phone, whistle, paperclip, flamingo, football helmet, eyeglasses.

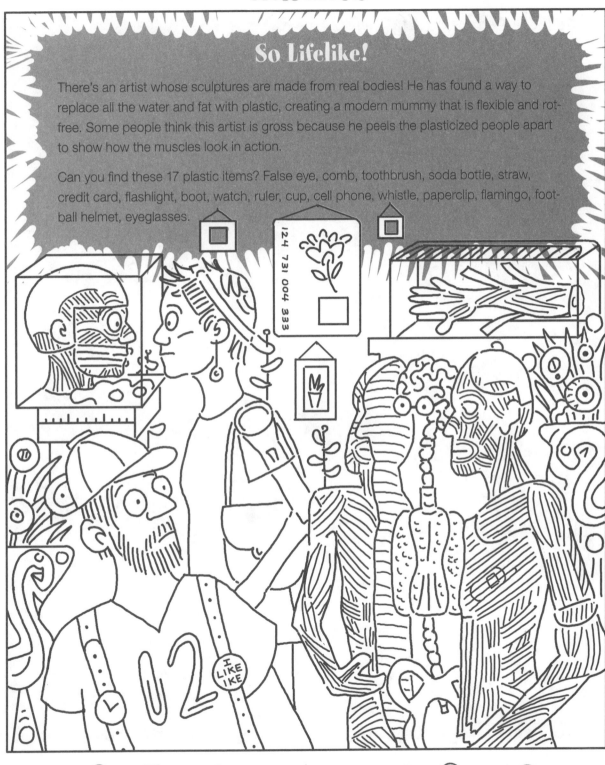

Creature Feature

A makeup artist works behind the scenes to help actors look their best. But how about a makeup artist who transforms normal actors into half-rotten zombies and slime-dripping aliens? These artists' work is made of fake blood, plastic skin, rubber guts, and all kinds of slippery goo.

Can you find the 10 hidden paintbrushes this artist will use to get these monsters looking really gross? See if you can find two extra eyeballs, too.

Take Out the Art

Sculptures are often made of wood, clay, or stone. You don't expect sculptures to be made from plastic bags filled with trash! Some artists photograph the bulging bags, while others display the actual trash in a gallery beside more traditional sculptures. One artist got mad when the janitor accidentally threw his artwork away!

Can you find these other works of garbage art? Empty milk carton, chicken wishbone, moldy slice of bread, half eggshell, used cotton swab, rotten fish, broken glass, empty can, one sneaker, plastic spoon.

The Fart as Art

Many artists play the flute. But how about a performer who could play a flute with his farts? Joseph Pujol was a Frenchman in the 1800s who could toot the flute, as well as do fart impressions of farm animals, thunderstorms, and cannon fire.

Monsieur Pujol often farted and recited a rhyme at the same time. Can you find six hearts, two darts, one work of art, and a fart chart?

Gross Artists

Polluted Paint

Many hundreds of years ago, each artist had their own special way of making paint. Some artists would mix the dry colors with oil. Others would mix the pigments with egg yolk. Sometimes they would also add earwax to make the paint smooth and get rid of tiny bubbles!

Can you find the 14 hidden cotton swabs Leonardo has used to get earwax?

Gross Gurning

Ever had an ugly face contest? You were "gurning." This word describes a folk art form in Britain. Gurners contort their faces to look extremely gross, crazy, or scary. They cross their eyes, suck in their cheeks, and stick their jaw out. Some "senior" gurners can even get their jaw up over their nose! You can try it, too, but it's easier if you have false teeth to take out.

At first glance, this is a lovely young woman looking at the moon. But look again! She has gurned herself into an ugly old woman! Keep looking. Can you find the old man, too?

Art Attack

In "live art" the actions of the artist are the work of art. It's often messy, and can get pretty gross. There are artists who paint with blood, eat poop, get objects stuck in their skin, and have food fights. Don't sit too close to live art in action!

Can you find two each of the following art objects being tossed in this food fight: slices of pizza, bowls of salad, rotten bananas, tomatoes, ice cream cones, fried eggs, pies, octopi.

APPENDIX A

Now where did I see that...?

You have already looked for more than 1,000 hidden objects, but you're not done yet! See if you can find each of these picture pieces somewhere in this book. Write the name of the puzzle each piece is from in the space under each box. HINT: There is only one picture piece from each chapter.

APPENDIX B

Resources

Haven't you had enough gross yet? No? Well then, here are a few of our favorite gross books and Web sites.

Books

Ripleys' Believe It or Not! Special Edition 2006

By Ripley Entertainment (2005). You'll find a whole cast of bizarre, amazing, and, of course, gross people in the latest collection from Ripley. Meet the man who is transforming himself into a lizard, a woman who makes portraits from animals she learned to stuff, and people who enjoy stuffing themselves into incredibly small places.

Poop

By Nicola Davies, illustrated by Neal Layton (2004). Everything you ever wanted to know about poop. Funny and informative, with great pictures that will keep you giggling even when you want to say "Eeeeew!" And remember, a whole bunch of people, including scientists, authors, and artists, made it their job to bring you this poop!

Make Your Own "Barf Buffet"

There are many cooks who specialize in recipes that are supposed to look disgusting! Here are two good collections that will help you whip up a Used Kitty Litter Cake or Hairy Eyeball Salad.

Family Fun Tricks and Treats: 100 Wickedly Easy Costumes, Crafts, Games & Foods

By Deanna F. Cook (by the editors of *Family Fun* magazine).

Gross Grub

By Cheryl Porter (Random House).

Hands-On Grossology

By Sylvia Branzei, illustrated by Jack Keely (2003). Want to do more than just deal with grossness on the printed page? You too can be a gross scientist! Here are over 30 experiments to let you get hands-deep in gross.

Gross Universe: Your Guide to All Disgusting Things Under the Sun

By Jeff Szpirglas (2004). A guide to many of the disgusting, yet amazing, things in our world, be it animal, plant, or human.

Web Sites

Remember, not all of these sites are designed just for kids. Go exploring with a parent so you don't end up somewhere that's not appropriate for you! Besides, don't you think your folks would appreciate a little quality gross time with you?

http://oceanlink.island.net/oinfo/hagfish/hagfishathome.html

Some science students got a little crazy, and tried baking scones using hagfish slime instead of eggs! Read what happened.

www.zoology.ubc.ca/~bwilson/herringsound.wav

Listen to an actual herring fart!

Resources

*www.uky.edu/Ag/Entomology/ythfacts/bugfood/
yf813.htm*

Read all about people who love to eat bugs! You
should definitely have the adult in your household who
cooks dinner read this article with you. Grasshopper
tacos, anyone?

www.amnh.org/nationalcenter/infection/

Get the facts on the "microbe hunters," those
daring doctors who examine diarrhea, snot, blood,
and all kinds of body rot to see what it is that makes
people sick. Solve a microbe mystery and follow the
lunch ladies to see what is getting into the cafeteria
food!

*www.extremescience.com/
GalleryofScientists.htm*

Learn about scientists such as Dr. Rivas, who trav-
els to the wetlands of Venezuela and searches bare-
foot through the mud until he feels a giant anaconda
snake.

www.guinnessworldrecords.com

Get lost here looking at the world records for strange
diseases, incredible body parts, and medical mar-
vels. Whether it is the champion eyeball popper, the
longest sneezing bout, or the person who can spit a
dead cricket the farthest, we guarantee you will be
fascinated!

PUZZLE ANSWERS

page 2 • **Ready, Set, Go?**

page 3 • **Rough Landing**

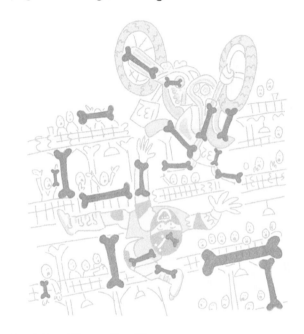

page 4 • **Play Ball!**

page 5 • **Throw the Dice**

Puzzle Answers

page 6 • Row, Row, Row Your Boat

page 7 • Blood & Sweat

page 8 • Lunch Overboard!

page 9 • Seeing Red

page 10 • **Uncle!!**

page 11 • **Round and Round You Go**

page 12 • **Bubble Trouble**

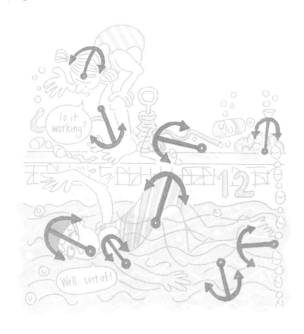

page 14 • **Space Poop**

Puzzle Answers

page 15 • **Foul Fugitives**

page 16 • **Candlelight Supper?**

page 17 • **Headaches**

page 18 • **Rock Snot**

page 19 • **Dinner Duo**

page 20 • **Yank!**

page 21 • **Head for Gold**

page 22 • **Snow Burn**

Puzzle Answers

page 23 • **Oh, Nuts!**

page 24 • **Not with Your Mouth Full!**

page 26 • **Rat Ho!**

page 27 • **Glub, Glub!**

page 28 • **Captain No Nose**

page 29 • **Nasty Nines**

page 30 • **Hard Life**

page 31 • **Fish Food**

Puzzle Answers

page 32 • **Cut on the Dotted Line**

page 33 • **Bilge Rats**

page 34 • **Oops!**

page 35 • **Move Over**

page 36 • **Smile?!**

page 38 • **WAIT! I Want a Haircut!**

page 39 • **Open Wide**

page 40 • **Slimy Helpers**

Puzzle Answers

page 41 • **Instant Finger, Just Add Toe**

page 42 • **Peculiari-tea**

page 43 • **Totally Tumors**

page 44 • **Potty Mouth**

page 45 • **Bark and Barf**

page 46 • **Eye Doctor**

page 47 • **Bug Bites**

page 48 • **Gross Anatomy**

Puzzle Answers

page 50 • **Ouch!**

page 51 • **Great Grease!**

page 52 • **Battle Scars**

page 53 • **Dirty Laundry**

page 54 • **Ready, Aim, THROW!**

page 55 • **Soldier's Soup**

page 56 • **Wild Warriors**

page 57 • **Food Bag**

Puzzle Answers

page 58 • **There She Blows!**

page 59 • **Clean Machine?**

page 60 • **What's the Rush?**

page 62 • **Wiggly Dinner**

page 63 • **Peanut Butter and Jellyfish**

page 64 • **2 Scoops of Goop**

page 65 • **Barf Buffet**

page 66 • **Glue Broth**

Puzzle Answers

page 67 • **On Top of Spaghetti?**

page 68 • **Slow Cooking**

page 69 • **Wanted Alive**

page 70 • **Scones with Slime**

page 71 • **Worm Cheese**

page 72 • **Sneaky Salad**

page 74 • **A Stitch in Time**

page 75 • **Sea Sick?**

Puzzle Answers

page 76 • Packed with Poop

page 77 • Packed with People

page 78 • Wicked Water

page 79 • Good to the Last Drop

page 80 • **Poopsicles**

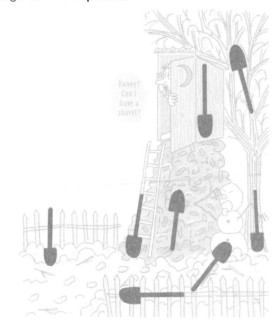

page 81 • **Flied Chicken**

page 82 • **Secret Ingredient**

page 83 • **House Call**

Puzzle Answers

page 84 • **The Clean Plate Club**

page 86 • **Sneak Peek**

page 87 • **Totally Tubular**

page 88 • **Finally!**

The EVERYTHING KIDS' Gross Hidden Pictures Book

page 89 • **Excuse You!**

page 90 • **Digging for Diapers**

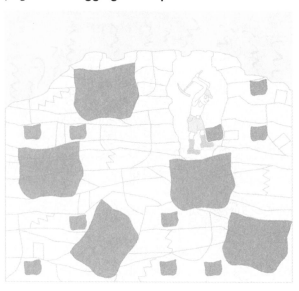

page 91 • **The Nose Knows**

page 92 • **Bathroom 101**

Puzzle Answers

page 93 • **Look Out Below!**

page 94 • **Rot Watch**

page 95 • **Come and Get It!**

page 96 • **The Vomit Comet**

page 98 • **Hairy Portrait**

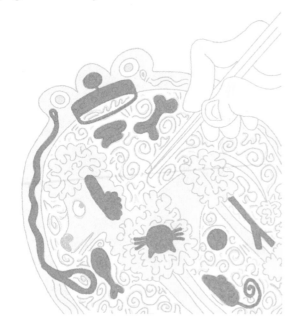

page 99 • **Petite Feet**

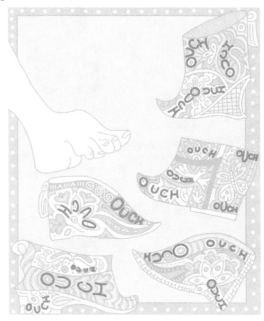

page 100 • **Play It Again, Slime**

page 101 • **So Lifelike!**

Puzzle Answers

page 102 • Creature Feature

page 103 • Take Out the Art

page 104 • The Fart as Art

page 105 • Polluted Paint

page 106 • **Ugh!**

page 107 • **Gross Gurning**

Old Woman

Old Man

page 108 • **Art Attack**

page 109 • **Now where did I see that...?**

1. Uncle!

2. Headaches

3. Oops!

4. Peculiari-tea

5. Great Grease!

6. 2 Scoops of Goop

7. Packed with Poop

8. The Vomit Comet

9. The Fart as Art

The Everything® Kids'
GROSS Series

Chock—full of sickening entertainment for hours of disgusting fun.

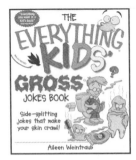

The Everything® Kids'
Gross Jokes Book
1-59337-448-8, $7.95

The Everything® Kids' Gross
Puzzle & Activity Book
1-59337-447-X, $7.95

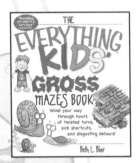

The Everything® Kids'
Gross Mazes Book
1-59337-616-2, $7.95

The Everything® Kids' Gross
Hidden Pictures Book
1-59337-615-4, $7.95